Praise for *Speedmailing*

'Smart people are lazy. So if you want to double your effectiveness and productivity emailing clients, colleagues and friends, read this book.'
Eelco Smit, personal and business coach for entrepreneurs and bestselling author, *Book for MEN*

'Simplicity is underestimated. Richard has sharpened the knife of day-to-day email management in the leanest possible way.'
Nick Bortot, founder and CEO, FinTech startup BUX

'Speedmailing is a concise action plan for mastering email. Richard has distilled thousands of hours of training into an easy to follow guide that will turn your inbox from a burden into a powerful business tool.'
Marshall Hughes, Inbox Zero Coach, coach.me

'Richard gives us a practical approach to email that really works, with useful habits and shortcuts that can drastically change the way we work. If you want to tame the monster that email has become, this book is for you. Forget emailing – the future is Speedmailing!'
Shirley Taylor, bestselling author, *Model Business Letters*, 7th Edition

'All my career I have focused on how we can get more leverage from our brain and process information quicker and better. Richard's way of dealing with email blew me away when I realised that I will spend less energy on a per email basis, today and every day from now on. What a return on investment!'
Mark Tigchelaar, CEO, UseClark and specialist in speed reading and productivity

'An easy and practical life changer, one of these books of which you think: "Why didn't I read that earlier? It would help me so much".'
Marine Guignardeau, Learning and Development Manager, L'Oréal Netherlands

'Until bots and AI solve the hassle of email, dealing with large quantities of email is a skill that is rarely mastered. This is definitely one of the best books on it and should be mandatory for every knowledge-worker.'
Martijn Aslander, speaker, writer and boardroom sparring partner

Speedmailing

PEARSON

At Pearson, we believe in learning – all kinds of learning for all kinds of people. Whether it's at home, in the classroom or in the workplace, learning is the key to improving our life chances.

That's why we're working with leading authors to bring you the latest thinking and the best practices, so you can get better at the things that are important to you. You can learn on the page or on the move, and with content that's always crafted to help you understand quickly and apply what you've learned.

If you want to upgrade your personal skills or accelerate your career, become a more effective leader or more powerful communicator, discover new opportunities or simply find more inspiration, we can help you make progress in your work and life.

Every day our work helps learning flourish, and wherever learning flourishes, so do people.

To learn more please visit us at: **www.pearson.com/uk**

Speedmailing
Turn your work enemy into your best work tool

Richard Wolfe

Harlow, England • London • New York • Boston • San Francisco • Toronto • Sydney • Auckland • Singapore • Hong Kong
Tokyo • Seoul • Taipei • New Delhi • Cape Town • São Paulo • Mexico City • Madrid • Amsterdam • Munich • Paris • Milan

PEARSON EDUCATION LIMITED
Edinburgh Gate
Harlow CM20 2JE
United Kingdom
Tel: +44 (0)1279 623623
Web: www.pearson.com/uk

First published 2016 (print and electronic)

ISBN: 978-1-292-14226-5 (print)
        978-1-292-14227-2 (PDF)
        978-1-292-14228-9 (ePub)

British Library Cataloguing-in-Publication Data
A catalogue record for the print edition is available from the British Library

Library of Congress Cataloging-in-Publication Data

Names: Wolfe, Richard, 1972- author.
Title: Speedmailing : turn your work enemy into your best work tool / Richard
  Wolfe.
Description: Harlow, United Kingdom : Pearson Education, 2016.
Identifiers: LCCN 2016022852 | ISBN 9781292142265 (pbk.)
Subjects: LCSH: Electronic mail systems. | Electronic mail messages. |
  Business communication.
Classification: LCC HE7551 .W65 2016 | DDC 651.7/402854692—dc23
LC record available at https://lccn.loc.gov/2016022852

10 9 8 7 6 5 4 3 2 1
20 19 18 17 16

Cover design by Two Associates

Print edition typeset in 9.5/13pt NeoSansPro by iEnergizer Aptara®, Ltd
Printed in Great Britain by Henry Ling Ltd, at the Dorset Press, Dorchester, Dorset

NOTE THAT ANY PAGE CROSS REFERENCES REFER TO THE PRINT EDITION

Contents

About the author

Richard is fascinated with how we create technology to increase our productivity and then often seem to achieve the opposite. He has a passion for finding easy ways to make technology work *for* us rather than *against* us.

After business school, and many years in the internet industry, Richard decided to dedicate himself to helping people use one of the most ubiquitous technologies around today: email. Because of the problems it created in our society, email ranges from a top three stress creator to a highly ignored medium.

Richard was born in Australia and grew up in the Netherlands. He is a pursuer of simplicity, which is reflected in the courses provided by his company, Email Handyman, the productivity app he developed called Braintoss, as well as the many life-hacks he inserts into the lives of his family, colleagues and fellow cricket players – and now also through his first publication, *Speedmailing*.

Many thanks

In no particular order I would like to thank everyone below for providing inspiration and/or help putting this book together:

Robert Wolfe	Jacklin Goverde
David Allen	Evert Jan Boon
Graham Alcott	Michiel Ploeger
Stephen Covey	Linda Kist
Seth Godin	Erwin Nelissen
Gina Trapani	Nienke Strikwerda
Merlin Mann	Sonia Harjani
Tim Feriss	Richard van Denderen
Taco Oosterkamp	Linnea Thomander
Jelle Hermus	Patrick Leenheers
Remco Verdonk	Zahid Malik
Iris van den Berg	Eloise Cook
Elysia Brenner	Pascal and the boys

Publisher's acknowledgements

The Apple logo and the iPhone® and iPad® names are trademarks of Apple Inc. All Apple screenshots reprinted with permission from Apple Inc. The Microsoft screenshots are reprinted by permission of Microsoft Corporation. The Android™ logo, Android™ and Gmail™ are trademarks of Google Inc.

We are grateful to the following for permission to use copyright material:

Photo on p. 10 © Jojje/Shutterstock; photos on pp. 32 and 35 © Melpomene/Shutterstock; photo on p. 33 © Andrew Paterson/Alamy Images.

Introduction

I am lazy. But if I say that to the people in my life, they laugh and tell me I'm one of the most energetic people they know. Some say they get tired just *watching* all the things I do. The truth is I'm a curious person – but I'd rather work smart than work hard. I avoid tedious activities, and I always look for the easiest way to do anything. Like I said, I'm lazy. So how do I fool my friends? It's simple, I just have a good system.

One of the greatest necessary evils of my life (and probably yours too) is email. It's an extremely useful and powerful tool . . . but it can easily become tedious – and you know now how I hate that. If we let them, our inboxes can take over our lives. Research done by McKinsey shows that we spend nearly one-third of our working hours reading and answering emails, and if that's not bad enough, a study done in the USA by Good Technology reveals that *50 per cent of working adults check email while still in bed*. We're getting lost in the piles of email taking over our working lives. We've traded actual productivity for immediate response times.

Does it in fact hurt? Research at CSD Loughborough University found that it takes an average of 64 seconds to recover from an email interruption. The *Harvard Business Review* paints a direr picture, estimating that it takes a total of 24 minutes to get back on task after opening an email. No wonder Gartner estimates that email overload costs about 12 per cent of wages. That's an expensive way to spend your time, whether you're working for yourself or someone else.

Nobody wants to spend their lives reading email – which is why I've come up with a system of email management that has not only decimated the amount of time I spend in my inbox, but one that also gives me a clearer overview of all of my to-dos. I call it 'speedmailing', and it's how I've turned my worst work enemy into my best work tool.

The method has worked so well for me that I've started teaching it to others who want to manage their email rather than letting it manage them. In addition to my online workshops, I now work with like-minded time-management experts to offer two-to-three-hour workshops to professionals in more than 15 countries around the world under the name 'Email Handyman'. Wondering what these workshops are about? In this book you'll learn the basics of the speedmailing method in under 30 minutes. You'll pick up a few simple habits and shortcuts that you can use for life that will drastically cut down on the time you spend on email PLUS give you a clearer overview of your tasks and to-dos. Whether you're lazy or just want to be more efficient, you will save time, giving you the freedom to spend your days the way you choose.

Speedmailing works well on any email program and you will find tips for Microsoft Outlook®, Apple Mail, Gmail™, iOS™, Android™, etc., throughout the book. To keep the book short and simple the first chapters mainly have screenshots of Outlook and the last chapter goes into detail on all popular devices and platforms.

Two-week trial
Not sure if this system is for you? We encourage you to try it out for two weeks – this book will have you ready to go in 30 minutes. All the changes we suggest are relatively simple, so it's easy to revert to your old system of email management if you don't find that, after two weeks, the speedmailing system has made your life easier and your emailing faster.

The benefits of speedmailing

- Empty inbox every day
- Increased productivity and peace of mind
- Your to-do list in one place
- A natural system of reminders
- Nothing slips through the cracks
- Better communication
- Less post-holiday stress

1 How to master your inbox

Tips and tricks

Speedmailing is all about shortcuts and simple tricks. So, while changing habits may *seem* difficult at first, the speed-mailing habits you learn here will quickly become second nature - and that's when you'll *really* notice the benefits. Much like upgrading your smartphone, it's a momentary pain to update all your data and apps and get used to the new interface, but that is soon outweighed by the awesome power of your new gadget.

So what are these tips and tricks? The speedmailing equation essentially boils down to:

5 steps to process incoming mail + 4 action folders + 3 golden rules = 0 emails in your inbox.

Paving the path to better email and task management also includes mastering your email client - especially the handy keyboard shortcuts that put the 'speed' in speedmailing. You'll find these highlighted throughout the book, with a complete overview in Chapter 5.

Five processing steps

We will introduce a way of working that's similar to a good clean-desk policy, in which your inbox has just one function: it's the place where new emails you haven't decided about reside. Nothing else. To get there, you need to effectively process the email in your inbox – which you can do in five simple steps:

1 Turn off pop-up email notifications.
2 Process your inbox just a couple of times a day.
3 Empty your inbox each time . . .
4 . . . by quickly sorting each email into one of four action-related folders (using keyboard shortcuts).
5 File all emails that no longer require your attention in a single folder.

Step 1: turn off pop-up email notifications

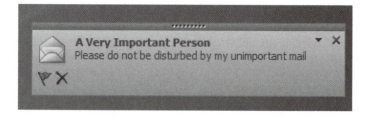

Most email programs will tell you when a new email arrives, preferably in as many ways as possible to make sure it doesn't escape your attention. Although it might seem smart to stay on top of the news as it comes in, it's actually pretty counter-productive – each notification is distracting you from the task at hand. In the end, neither the email nor the thing you were working on is getting your full attention. It's a lose-lose situation. So turn off your email notifications (on your mobile devices, too) – think of it as sanity security. The email will be there waiting for you when you have time to give it your undivided attention.

So how do we turn notifications off? See Chapter 5 for all the ins and outs of managing mail in Outlook, Gmail and other email programs.

Step 2: process your inbox just a couple of times a day

The clear follow-up question is: without the alerts, when *should* you check your email?

Ideally, just *a couple of times per day* (for example, first thing in the morning and after lunch) – whenever you do it, give it your undivided attention. Process the emails in one go, and then get on with your most important tasks. Try not to check too frequently, or you'll just end up losing time again by getting sucked back into email enthrallment.

Many of you will object that it's just not possible in your job to check your email only a couple of times a day. However, I'd counter it's just not possible to do your job well if you check your email continuously. Reducing the amount of times you check your mail will increase your productivity. And, *if it's really urgent, it shouldn't be managed through email* in the first place!

Our email culture has created an expectation of immediate response – or, at least, we seem to think it has. In actuality, we are often away from our desks, and unable to respond to emails for hours at a time. (Sometimes we're even too busy to check our smartphones.) Our clients and co-workers know that, if they need to speak to us immediately, they are better off picking up the phone. Emails are generally saved for non-urgent tasks. You should operate by the same principle: if it's really important or time sensitive, don't rely on email alone.

Plus, *you don't need to create an expectation of immediate response*. You can't always be available the moment an email comes in, or sometimes you want to think an email over a little before responding. That's fine. Your customers and colleagues will be better served by your *increased productivity* than by hearing back from you the moment they've sent you an email.

Pro tip
Do make sure you respond to every email within two working days, even if it is just to inform the person you will get back to them later! If you won't be checking your email for more than two working days, remember to turn on your 'out-of-office assistant' ('vacation responder' in Gmail).

Step 3: empty your inbox each time

In the next section we'll look at *how* exactly you'll be sorting your email, but the important thing to know for now is that at the end of the process you will be looking at an empty inbox a few times per day. Yep, it's as satisfying as it sounds.

This means that you shouldn't leave a single email in your inbox when you're done processing. Just start from the top and sort, sort, sort - every email fits into one of the four folders described in the next step.

Emptying your inbox on your mobile device is just as easy if the folders are set up correctly. Moving an email from your inbox to one of the folders can be done on all common mobile platforms. Both the setting up of the folders and how to move an email on your mobile is explained in Chapter 5.

Step 4: sort emails into four action-related folders

You obviously can't take care of every email in your inbox in one sitting – not if your inbox looks like mine, anyway! So, we need a way to prioritise our mail and make sure we (a) don't miss any emails (or see them too late) and (b) don't lose track of the to-dos they contain.

To implement a 'clean-mailbox policy' that will allow you to focus on your most important tasks, we need to introduce a few folders to help you quickly and effectively sort the email that comes in. These folders are time-based, and not subject-based; subject-based categorisation quickly gets too complex to manage efficiently, especially as content categories change over time. The most effective way to sort emails is based on how soon they require your attention. I recommend four 'action folders':

1 **Do this week.** This is your to-do list. File any email that is urgent and/or important enough to be done in the short term (as in, within a week), but cannot be done in two minutes (more on the two-minute rule in a bit). This includes emails that have to be taken care of today!

2 **Holding for later.** This is a parking spot for emails that require your attention but are less urgent. Anything that can be done a week from now or later should be parked here for later review. When in doubt, put it here. Once a week this folder should be reviewed to determine which emails need to become to-do items.

3 **Waiting for others.** This folder contains emails you need to keep an eye on, but the ball is in someone else's court. While you are waiting for an answer or resolution, the mail should wait here. Again, review this folder once a week.

4 **Calendar.** Technically this isn't really a folder but a feature of your email client. It's where any date-specific

emails should be filed. You can save the entire email here, so that you have all the details. If you need to block time to prepare for a meeting or complete the task, create a calendar appointment for yourself to do that.

By emptying your inbox a couple of times a day you will be on top of all the news without becoming a slave of your inbox. Once empty, you will find your new and improved task list, 'Do This Week', to be a good spot to work from. It is a list of emails, each one represents a task related to it and as the list does not change unless you add or remove new ones yourself, it does not distract you the way your inbox does. As you complete tasks from your 'Do This Week' folder you can 'tick them off' by moving them to 'Filed Items'. Doing this with the keyboard shortcuts explained in Chapter 5 will turn you into a true speedmailer.

> 📧 You can drag an email onto the Calendar button in Outlook (bottom-left) to create a new appointment which includes a copy of the text of the email in the notes field. This also works for saving the sender as a contact: just drag the email onto the Contacts button.

> **Pro tip**
> Use this process to manage all your to-dos! Whenever you think of something you need to do, you can simply email it to yourself and process that task like the rest. I've developed a reminder app to make this process even simpler: Braintoss lets you email yourself a quick text, voice message, or photo reminder with the push of a button. David Allen named Braintoss 'the best GTD® capture tool for the iPhone®'. His book, *Getting Things Done*, is the guiding principle to the speedmailing method.

Step 5: file all emails that no longer need your attention in a single folder

Once you've finished with an email, you'll often want to keep it to look up or refer to later. You might be tempted to create a complicated hierarchy of folders by projects, customers, or events to sort and save these old emails – but trust me, that's a waste of time. Building and updating all these folders will take more time than you actually spend on the email, and the more complicated the structure, the more problems it can cause when trying to retrieve the emails we need down the track.

Far better to use a single filing folder. For one, this ensures your folder structure will never be out of date! Some email clients like Gmail already have this functionality built in, allowing you to simply use an archiving button to file emails. If your email client doesn't offer this option, it's simple to make your own: just by adding one more folder ('Filed Items') to your action folders.

You may get a little nervous about putting all your email messages in a single folder. 'How am I ever going to find anything?', I hear you ask. The key to this single-filing method is your email client's search function. In fact, your email's search bar is one of the most powerful speedmailing tools at your fingertips. Later, we'll look in detail at how you can harness the power of your email client's search capabilities.

2 The ground rules of speedmailing

Now that you know the five basic steps to start speedmailing, let's set some ground rules for making this process as effective and efficient as possible.

The three golden rules

1 Empty your inbox one email at a time - and no putting back - making quick decisions and using keyboard shortcuts.
2 If it can be done in two minutes, do it immediately!
3 Check all your action folders weekly.

1. One email at a time - think quickly and use shortcuts

The point of speedmailing is obviously to be as quick as possible - and sorting should be the speediest part of the process.

Your inbox should be a conveyor belt, and you a sorting machine. Don't look for the special emails – the interesting or important ones. That's how you lose time, looking over less important emails again and again as you search. Simply process *all* emails from the top, one at a time. You can address the quick ones on the go. (We'll talk about the two-minute rule in a moment.) Sort all the others into their rightful action folder so you can attend to them in due time. Once you have finished sorting, you will have all your important emails in one place, and you'll be ready to start knocking out your to-dos with maximum efficiency.

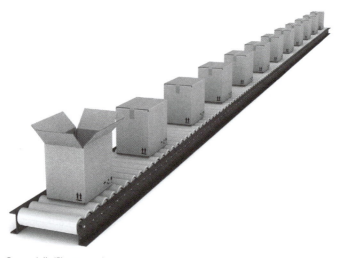

Source: Jojje/Shutterstock

I find it helps to consider yourself in a different role when you enter your inbox. I use the postman metaphor, and visualise putting on a postman hat when starting on my inbox. When I am finished sorting and my inbox is empty, I take it off again and go back to my tasks. A bit weird perhaps, but it works well!

Working this way is not only efficient, but it tackles the most recent emails first – meaning that you can often just ignore older related emails lower in the list. By going through the list in order, you will also get into a flow of decision making and reduce the time spent on each email. Better yet, when your brain goes into autopilot mode, your decision making speed improves and you actually consume less energy. The very definition of efficiency!

When you open an email, simply ask yourself, 'Do I have to act on this email? Is there something *I* have to do?' If the answer is yes but the task cannot be done in two minutes, ask yourself if you need to do it today or this week. If it's a yes again, it goes in 'Do This Week'. If there's a specific date you need to act, save the email to your Calendar. Otherwise you should park it in 'Holding for Later'. When in doubt, put it in 'Holding for Later' and revisit it in your weekly review. (More on that in a moment.)

If the email is *not* waiting for an action from you, then you have three options: delete, file/archive, or sort into 'Waiting for Others'. Just delete anything you know is rubbish or you don't need – note that the keyboard's Delete key will do this automatically. See Chapter 5 for more shortcuts you can use to speed up the process in Outlook and Gmail.

It should take no more than *10–15 minutes to completely empty your inbox* this way. Especially if you embrace using keyboard shortcuts to move emails from your inbox to the required folder. In Outlook this shortcut is Ctrl+Shift+V, followed by typing the first letter of the folder name and then pressing Enter. This sequence seems hard in the beginning, but within days, if not hours, it will become a speedy habit which costs less time and energy than using the mouse.

The second component of the first golden rule is that there is no putting back into your inbox any emails that

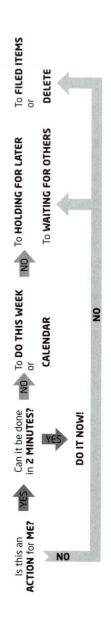

Is this an **ACTION** for **ME?**

YES

Can it be done in **2 MINUTES?**

YES → **DO IT NOW!**

NO → To **DO THIS WEEK** or **CALENDAR**

NO → To **HOLDING FOR LATER**

To **WAITING FOR OTHERS**

NO

To **FILED ITEMS** or **DELETE**

NO

have been sorted. Once you have decided what to do with an email, it will be banished to one of the action folders. Perhaps it will move between folders, but never back to the inbox. This ensures that your inbox contains *only* new emails you haven't yet seen, allowing you to empty it and get focused faster.

2. Follow the two-minute rule

If the answer to the question 'Do I have to act on this?' is YES and the task can be done quickly, move on to the second golden rule, the *two-minute rule.*

As you sort through your inbox, you'll find many emails that need only a brief answer or question in return, or just a quick retrieval of information. Others are simply short news-letters or a to-do that can immediately be forwarded to someone else. Whatever it is, if it will take less than two minutes to do it, take care of it immediately. It's amazing how many to-dos you can quickly check off your list in this way.

This simple rule can cut your task list in half or more in just the 10-15 minutes it takes to sort your mail, with the bonus of the motivational boost that comes with getting a lot of little stuff done. Now you're ready to go tackle the big to-dos.

When I am processing my inbox on my mobile I turn the two-minute rule into a 20-second rule. Quick and easy ones I will do, but if an email needs a little more attention and correct typing then I will move it to my 'Do This Week' folder on my mobile so I can deal with it later when I am back behind my computer.

3. Review all folders once a week

The weekly check is a recurring calendar appointment you make for yourself to get a handle on the state of your to-dos. You'll check all your folders, paper notes, etc., *rearranging priorities*, reminding yourself of the items that have slipped your mind, getting ready for the week ahead and closing off the week behind. As I've already mentioned, *this weekly check is your safety net*, catching items that slip through your own fingers or through other people's hands.

Most people like to do the weekly check at the end of the week, but make sure you leave enough time to address any necessary action items. We recommend scheduling it for Friday morning, in a place and at a time you won't be bothered. True, you might not make your appointment *every* week – but make sure you never skip two! Also carve out some time after your check to take care of the lost-and-found to-dos you absolutely must tackle before the weekend.

Your weekly checklist should include:

- **Calendar, past week.** Go through all your recently completed (or missed!) appointments to remind yourself of any actions you still need to take care of. Address those that can be completed within two minutes, or send an email reminder to yourself to be sorted into the appropriate action folder.

- **Calendar, coming week.** Go through all your upcoming appointments and see if any of them require extra attention prior to the meeting. If so, schedule yourself time for those activities or, if you are waiting on someone else, remind them about what you are waiting for.

- **Voicemails.** Now is also a good time to check your voicemail for any missed or saved messages. If any of them leads to an action point, send the action point to yourself as an email to be sorted the next time you process your inbox. (The Braintoss app is perfect for this.)

- **Paper notes.** Check any notebooks, Post-its, or loose pieces of paper you might have scrawled notes on this week for hidden action items. By converting them to email they become part of your system.

- **Do this week.** Check your 'Do This Week' folder for any pending items that really need to be resolved. For each item, decide to either reprioritise (move it to 'Holding for Later' or your archive), delegate (forward it to someone with a request, then move it to 'Waiting for Others'), or do it today. If it needs to be taken care of that day, mark the email as a high priority (you could use the red flag) and make sure to finish it.

- **Holding for later.** Check 'Holding for Later' to see if you need to get started on any of the items there within the next week. If so, move the email to 'Do This Week'. Often you will find items that no longer require your attention and can be filed.

- **Waiting for others.** Conclude by checking all items in 'Waiting for Others'. Hopefully most have been completed and can be filed, but if an item has not been resolved and you're still waiting for someone or something else, leave the email in the 'Waiting for Others' folder and send the person you're waiting on a reminder – keeping in mind that calling or stopping by their desk will generally get results faster!

The processing steps and golden rules in action

Let's have a quick rerun of the five processing steps on a real inbox, taking into account the golden rules. Here is my own mailbox with new emails. Let's deal with them one at a time, starting from the top (first golden rule).

In this first email, I am asked to meet next Tuesday. If I agree to attend, the answer to 'Do I have to act?' is yes, it cannot be done in two minutes (I have to wait until next Tuesday), so I commit this task to my Calendar. This can be done quickly by (a) replying with a meeting request using the small button next to Forward or (b) adding the mail to only my own Calendar. This is done by dragging the email onto the Calendar button at the bottom left. Both methods will bring up a new meeting dialogue with a copy of the text of the email in the notes part of the meeting.

After I have committed the task to my Calendar I can move the email to the 'Filed Items' folder using Ctrl+Shift+V, 1, Enter. The email is moved and I am already on the next email ready to make my next decision.

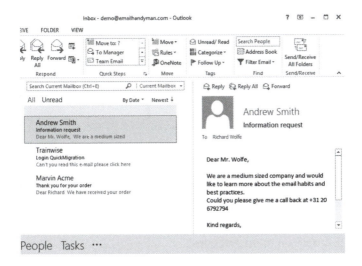

The next email is an information request about my company. Something I would like to do soon but cannot do in two minutes (second golden rule). Now I have to prioritise if this should be done within a week or later. In this case I choose to put it in my 'Do This Week' folder and attend to it later today or tomorrow (Ctrl+Shift+V, 2, Enter). And automatically I jump to the next email in my inbox.

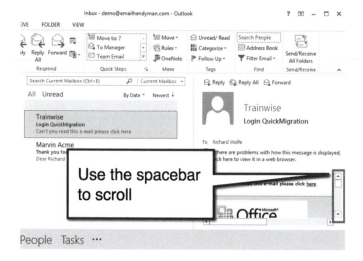

The next email gives me access to an online training course I really would like to follow but not right now. So for now I am going to move it to the 'Holding for Later' folder (Ctrl+Shift+V, 3, Enter). On to the last email.

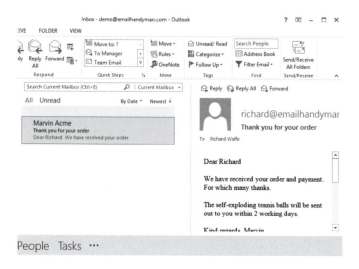

A lot of emails originate from systems that we work with or interact with online. This is a confirmation of an online order. And as I have already spent my money but am waiting for delivery I will move this email to 'Waiting for Others'. To be checked at the end of the week if all went well.

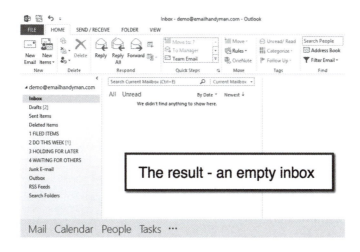

By using the folders to identify if an email still deserves your attention you have created a very simple task management system, so simple you can actually do your daily maintenance from your mobile phone. There is no need to use flags or colouring. Do note that a task should really only be in one spot at a time. It has to be done (a) at a specific time = Calendar, or (b) soon = 'Do This Week', or (c) sometime later perhaps = 'Holding for Later', or (d) by someone else = 'Waiting for Others' or (e) not anymore, it's done = 'Filed Items'.

Some examples:

What is the email about?	Where does it go?
New meeting next week	Copy to Calendar and then 'Filed Items'
Quick question	Answer in two minutes and then 'Filed Items'
Request for proposal	'Do This Week'
Boring newsletter or spam	Trash*
Relevant newsletter	Read in two minutes and then File or Delete
Conference confirmation	Copy to Calendar and then 'Filed Items'
Nice to read report	'Holding for Later'
Online purchase confirmation	'Waiting for Others'
CC mail from team member	Quick scan and then 'Filed Items'

It is definitely worthwhile scrolling down and unsubscribing in one or two clicks before deleting.

So now your inbox is empty. And of course this was a demo example with only four emails but even with 20 or 50 emails this process will not take long and you will notice most emails are filed or deleted. Once your inbox is empty you can return to your 'Do This Week' folder and start working on the emails that deserve your attention.

Lifesaver rule: the 'back from holiday' crunch

Unlike the other guidelines we've discussed in this chapter, the 'back from holiday' crunch isn't a rule for processing your email on a regular basis, but rather a simple method to get you through the mountains of mail that wait for you when you return to the office after being away for a few days or even weeks. The idea is to get you up to speed on everything you missed as quickly as possible without going crazy or losing an entire day to email. (You can also use this method to get through your backed-up inbox the first time you try speedmailing.)

The 'back from holiday' crunch uses the same principles you've already learned: emails are still sorted into four action folders one at a time. However, in the 'back from holiday' crunch, two extra rules apply:

1 Ignore the two-minute rule.
2 Apply the law of getting bored twice.

Simply start at the top of your emails and start sorting. However, even if an email can be done in two minutes, don't start on it but move it to 'Do This Week' instead. Trim down your processing time by being more selective about which tasks you take on. For example, do you really need to catch up on every newsletter you missed while you were away? You'll save yourself a lot of time if you delete with abandon – you're unlikely to miss it.

As you sort, you'll gradually notice that the emails you're reading feel less and less relevant. We call this getting bored. Rather than getting bored we want you to be getting back to work. Speed up the speedmailing process and prevent yourself from numbing your mind, when you've just returned to office life, by following the 'law of getting bored twice'. It essentially breaks down into a three-part process:

1 Once you get bored with sorting one by one from the top, switch to scanning for important emails (this only applies to the 'back from holiday' crunch!), and sort just those.
2 Once you get bored a second time, select all remaining emails (Ctrl+A) and file or archive them. If needed, you can always find them later using your search tool.
3 Now proceed to 'Do This Week' and start tackling your two-minute tasks. You're back working as usual already!

While it *is* possible that you will miss an older action item or two working this way, the speed of the crunch procedure more than makes up for these generally understandable slips with a drastic reduction in the time it takes to get you back to actual productivity. You'll be back impressing your boss and colleagues on the work floor the very morning you return!

3 Search: a speedmailer's best friend

If you ever waste time slogging through pages of old emails looking for a piece of information or the details of an agreement, you need to get (better) acquainted with your email client's search function. It will soon be your best friend.

Your email client's excellent ability to search (its built-in Google functionality, so to speak) is why we can get away with using such a simple, streamlined speedfiling structure. You can easily find any email, as long as you know what you are looking for.

Here's how to maximise the power of your searches.

Kick off your search with Ctrl+E (or Ctrl+F)

Even your searching can be speedy with the right shortcuts, and it's a good way to get in the habit of using keyboard shortcuts in general. Also, in programs like Outlook, where the search bar appears in different spots on different screens, Ctrl+E (Outlook) or Ctrl+F (most other programs) saves you time tracking it down.

You can also use the search tool in your Calendar or Contacts. Again, just type Ctrl+E or Ctrl+F and the name of the appointment or person you are seeking (or the location or anything else you remember about the meeting or contact) and you will receive a short list of all meeting/contacts that contain that word.

 Pro tip

Mobile phones often only synchronise emails for a selected period, like a week. Check the settings of your email account to see if you can increase it to a month. This will improve the chance of finding emails quickly on your mobile.

The spacebar is your biggest search friend

This may sound odd, but the most efficient search keyword in Outlook is a space. Often people only use one word or name to search, but when you use more words you get much more tailored results - exponentially more precise with each word you add. The right word combination will make it a lot easier to dig up the right emails. Use at least two words, which do not need to be a phrase or occur in any particular order. The more specific the words you use, the better. You will get more precise results if you search for 'quarterly review' rather than 'meeting'. But use whatever you can think of off the top of your head and don't waste time looking up. Do mind your spelling, though. The search function looks for exactly what you're asking.

Keep in mind that Outlook searches *all* of the following elements:

- The subject field
- Name fields
- Date fields
- The body of the email (text)
- Searchable attachments*

*If you have activated indexing in your email client.

This means that, if you can remember words from the text or even attachments, you can use that as part of your search query. This can be very helpful if you know product codes or invoice numbers that make the email you're searching for relatively unique.

Try to search for email the same way you would search the internet. If you can't remember the subject or someone's name, don't break your head over it! Just use the words you can remember from the email or attachment, just as if the email is a website that you need to find using Google!

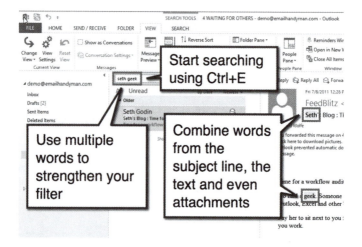

Start searching using Ctrl+E

Combine words from the subject line, the text and even attachments

Use multiple words to strengthen your filter

Too many and the minus trick

Sometimes you'll find that your search results are clogged by other similar-sounding emails from a certain source (like newsletters) or name. In these cases, you can add a minus sign (also known as a hyphen) to the front of a word you would like to *exclude from your search results.* (Note: 'football' without a space is similar to 'football' but 'foot -ball' with a space in the middle equals 'foot NOT ball'. And guess what, this trick also works in Google!)

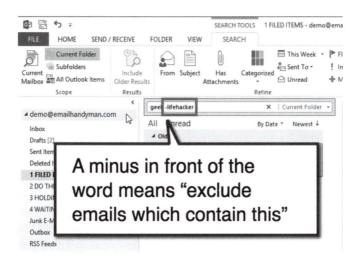

Outlook users can tailor their searches even more by using the search ribbon that only appears in search mode. For example, you can click the attachment button to eliminate all emails that do not have an attachment – which is very handy if you are searching for a file rather than an email!

Too few or still too many

Now, what if you have entered a couple of good search terms and still can't find the email you are looking for? Check the search scope to see if you are searching just one folder or all of them. By expanding your scope to 'All Folders' you avoid having to think about where the email may be filed.

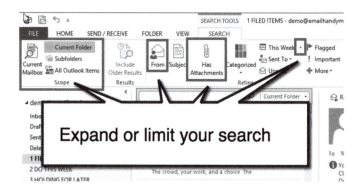

Expand or limit your search

If the results are still way too many and you have run out of words to add you can use the search ribbon to improve your filter. Some of my favourites are 'From' or 'To', 'Attachments' (if you are looking for one) and the little arrow next to 'This Week' (so you can search for emails from this month or last year).

Turn on conversation view

Conversation view: Gmail is known for it, and even Outlook has offered it since version 2010. More importantly, it can save you a lot of time and sorting hassle. Conversation view is turned off by default in Outlook (you can turn it on in the View tab), as it can be a bit confusing for people who aren't used to it. Yet for many people it can be a real time-saver to have all emails from a conversation gathered together in one thread (regardless of where they are filed). This is especially handy if you need to check the history of the conversation.

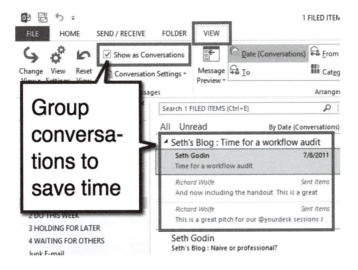

Pro tip

If you use conversation view and you file or delete the most recent email, the rest of the conversation might jump to a different spot in your inbox or folder (to the time of the next-most-recent email in the conversation). Also note that, if you change the email subject, it will start a new thread – and in some clients, different threads with the same subject might be combined.

4 The dos and don'ts of speedmailing

Now that you've got the basics of the system, I have a few final thoughts for you before you begin your speedmailing adventure. Beyond just sorting mail, your inbox management system should incorporate these dos and don'ts for speedier emailing that will make your life easier and keep your contacts happy.

When receiving email

Source: Melpomene/Shutterstock

- Check your email no more than a couple of times per day.
- Turn off all pop-up email notifications.
- Answer each email within two working days, or inform the sender that you will get back to them later.
- If you won't be able to respond to emails for two or more working days, turn on your 'out-of-office assistant'/'vacation responder'.

When sending email

Source: Andrew Paterson/Alamy Stock Photo

- Make sure the subject is clear and informative. Remember the receiver will want to be able to find it quickly later.

- If you regularly send the same or similar emails to different people, store a version in your Drafts folder so you don't have to rewrite it each time.

- Be polite, but get to the point and use clear language.

- Know when NOT to use email - when emotions or conflicts are involved or there is urgency.

- If it's important, don't rely on email alone.

Pro tip

Use the '80÷20 subject rule' when sending email. This means your subject line should clarify at least 80 per cent of the email's content for your reader(s). For example, 'Meeting about third-quarter returns' is much better than just 'Meeting' - it tells the person what to expect in the email and helps you both find it more easily later using the search function. In general, improving your email's subject line will result in quicker responses and less misunderstanding.

When replying to email

Source: Melpomene/Shutterstock

- Limit use of CC and especially 'Reply to All'.

- When you think someone else should see a discussion, forward it with an explanation of why you think it is relevant to them. Don't make them search the email history to try to figure it out. And, again, don't CC them if they only need to know the outcome of the discussion.

- Don't use an existing email thread to start a new topic (or at least change the subject line).

- When in doubt, wait a little while before composing your response (you can place the email in 'Do This Week' or 'Drafts'). Especially if it's something important or sensitive.

Inbox management tips

- Make your inbox cleaner (and give yourself less work) by unsubscribing from any newsletters you don't read regularly.

- If you have a mailbox limit, learn about your archiving options so you don't have to invest time in cleaning up old emails.

- Follow the same guidelines when checking email from your smartphone – except the two-minute rule becomes the 20-second rule.

Set your 'Do This Week' folder to display the number of emails inside (see 'Add the action folders' in Chapter 5), but not any of your other folders (which would become too distracting).

5 How to start speedmailing on your device or platform

So now you have all the tools you need to begin processing your email in a new way, a way that allows you to have an empty inbox on a daily basis. But how do you get started? This chapter contains step-by-step explanations on how to configure your email client for optimal emailing.

Speedmailing in Outlook

Turn off new email notifications

1 In Outlook, go to the **File** tab.
2 Choose **Options** from the menu.
3 Click on **Mail** in the menu on the left.
4 Untick all options in the **Message arrival** section.

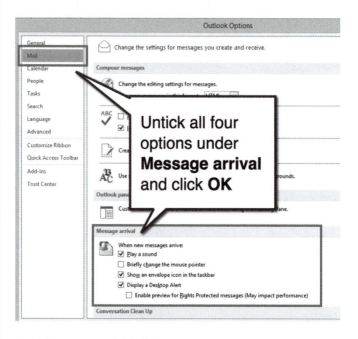

Archive your old folders

Already have a hierarchy of files to sort your email in place?
No need to fuss with them – just retire them all together as
they are. You can use your search function to find anything
you need later.

It's smart to check with your IT helpdesk how best to
archive old email. You might choose to move your old folders

to existing **Archive folders** (sometimes called Personal folders), but if your company has a central archiving system, you can leave your old folders in your **Mailbox**. If this is the case we suggest you stash the folders in a separate folder, which we will call **Zipped Folders**.

1 Create a folder called **Zipped Folders** by right-clicking on your mailbox (email address) and selecting **Add new folder**.
2 Move your existing folders to **Zipped Folders**. You will have to drag your folders in one by one. (Subfolders will be moved as well. If you have a lot of folders, it helps to start with the bottom folder.)

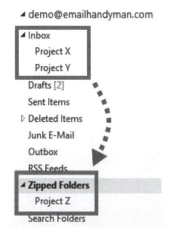

Add the action folders

1 In Outlook, go to **Mail** and in the folder list *right-click* on the mailbox at the top of your list (not your inbox, but the top level, which typically shows your *own email address*).
2 In the menu, choose **Add new folder**.
3 Type **1 FILED ITEMS** as the folder name and hit enter.

4 Repeat this to add the folders **2 DO THIS WEEK**, **3 HOLDING FOR LATER** and **4 WAITING FOR OTHERS**.

When completed, *right-click* the **Do This Week** folder and choose **Properties**. Under the Description box tick **Show total number of items** radio button to display all email (regardless of whether they are read or unread) in your to-do mailbox.

◢ demo@emailhandyman.com

Inbox
Drafts [2]
Sent Items
▷ Deleted Items

1 FILED ITEMS
2 DO THIS WEEK
3 HOLDING FOR LATER
4 WAITING FOR OTHERS

Junk E-Mail
Outbox
RSS Feeds
▷ Zipped Folders
Search Folders

Enter the weekly check into your Calendar

1 In Outlook, go to **Calendar** and select a time slot to do your weekly check (for instance, 9:00 AM to 9:30 AM Friday morning).

2 Enter **Email Weekly Check** as the subject of the appointment.

3 Click on **Recurrence** and hit Enter (it will recur weekly by default).

4 In the **Notes** field type (or copy and paste using Ctrl+C and Ctrl+V) the checklist below, and then save the appointment.

Weekly checklist

- Calendar, past week.
- Calendar, coming week.
- Voicemail and Paper notes.
- Do This Week.
- Holding for Later.
- Waiting for Others.

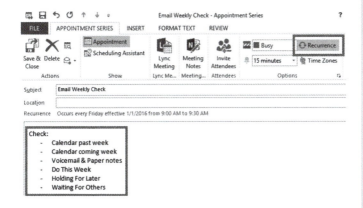

Top 10 keyboard shortcuts for Outlook

- (Shift) **Space** => read mail in preview pane.
- **Ctrl+Shift+V** => move mail.
- **Ctrl+E** => search.
- **Ctrl+N** => compose.
- **Ctrl+R** => reply.
- **Ctrl+Shift+R** => reply to all.
- **Ctrl+F** => forward.
- **Ctrl+Enter** => send.
- **Ctrl+Z** => undo last action.
- **Ctrl+1/2/3** => show email/calendar/contacts.

More keyboard shortcuts and a printable Tipbar for Outlook can be found on http://shortcuts.emailhandyman.com

 Pro tip

If you notice that the new email counter on your inbox folder is distracting you it is time to fix that for once and for all. This can be done by creating an Outlook Rule with the following criteria: **New rule on messages I receive - through the specified account** (step 2: confirm your account) **- mark it as read**. This may feel chaotic in the beginning, but the return is more focus and concentration on the tasks at hand!

Speedmailing in Apple Mail

Turn off new email notifications

1 In Mail, go to the **Preferences**.
2 Under **General** change the **New messages sound** to **None**.

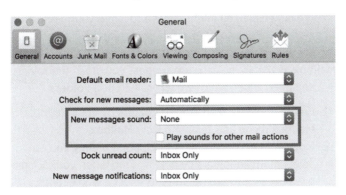

1 Now open the **System Preferences** and go to **Notification Center**.
2 Turn off *all* notifications for the Mail app.

Archive your old folders

Already have a hierarchy of files to sort your email in place? No need to fuss with them - just retire them all together as they are. You can use your search function to find anything you need later.

It's smart to check with your IT helpdesk how best to archive old email. You might choose to move your old folders to existing **archive folders**, but if your company has a central archiving system, you can leave your old folders in your **Mailbox**. If this is the case we suggest you stash the folders in a separate folder, which we will call **Zipped Folders**.

1 Create a folder called **Zipped Folders** by going to the **Mailbox** menu and selecting **New Mailbox**.
2 Move your existing folders to **Zipped Folders**. You can select multiple folders by holding **Cmd** when you click or, even better, by holding **Shift** to select a whole range. Then drag the folders onto **Zipped Folders**.

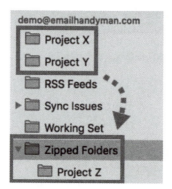

Add the action folders

1 In Mail, go to the **Mailbox** menu.
2 In the menu, choose **Add new folder**.

3 Type **1 FILED ITEMS** as the folder name and hit Enter (make sure **Location** is the name of your account).

1 Repeat this to add the folders **2 DO THIS WEEK**, **3 HOLDING FOR LATER** and **4 WAITING FOR OTHERS**.

The process of moving emails to the action folders can of course be done with a mouse or trackpad. But ideally (to reach ultimate speedmailing) you would use keyboard shortcuts. This can be done by making the action folders the first four folders on the **Favorites bar**: simply drag them one by one into the right spot.

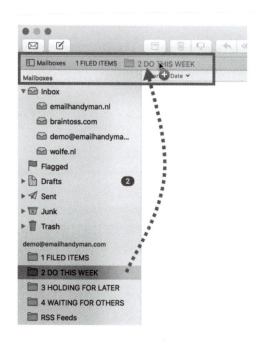

Then you can use the **Move to Favorite Mailbox** shortcut keys to move email from your inbox to an action folder by pressing **Cmd+Ctrl+1**, etc.

This method works really well if you have one email account. For multiple email accounts on Mail we recommend looking into a plugin named **MsgFiler**.

Enter the weekly check into your Calendar

1 Go to **Calendar** and select a time slot to do your weekly check (for instance, 9:00 AM to 10:00 AM Friday morning).
2 Enter **Email weekly check** as the subject of the event.
3 Click on **Repeat** then **Every Week**.
4 In the **Add Notes** field type (or copy and paste using Cmd+C and Cmd+V) the checklist below, and then save the appointment.

Weekly checklist

- Calendar, past week.
- Calendar, coming week.
- Voicemail.
- Paper notes.
- Do This Week.
- Holding for Later.
- Waiting for Others.

Apple Mail

Email weekly check ▣ ˅
Add Location

01 Jan 2016 09:00 to 10:00
Repeats Weekly
Alert 15 minutes before start (default)
Add Alert, Repeat, or Travel Time

Add Invitees

Check:
- Calendar past week
- Calendar coming week
- Voicemail & Paper notes
- Do This Week
- Holding For Later
- Waiting For Others

Add Attachment...

Speedmailing in Gmail ✉

In Gmail we recommend deactivating the smart inboxes to go back to having all your new email in one spot. This is done in **Settings** and then **Inbox**.

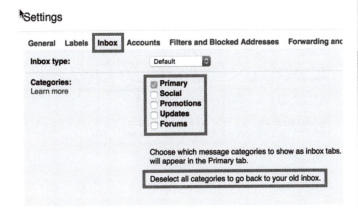

If you are using Inbox by Google, the setup is similar to Gmail. Even though you could achieve a 'smarter' version using the Snooze feature we still recommend working with Labels to sort your email quickly by hand.

Turn off new email notifications

1 In Gmail, go to **Settings**.
2 In the **General** settings scroll down to **Desktop Notifications**.
3 Set to **Mail notifications off**.

Settings

Gmail

General Labels Inbox Accounts Filters and Blocked Addresses Forwarding and PC
grouped together)

Send and Archive: Learn more	○ **Show "Send & Archive" button in reply** ● **Hide "Send & Archive" button in reply**
Undo Send:	☑ **Enable Undo Send** Send cancellation period: 10 ⬦ seconds
Stars:	**Drag the stars between the lists.** The stars will rotate in the search, hover your mouse over the image. **Presets:** **1 star** 4 stars all stars **In use:** ☆ **Not in use:** ★ ★ ★ ★ ☆ █ ▶ ❗
Desktop Notifications: (allows Email Handyman Mail to display popup notifications on your desktop when new email messages arrive) Learn more	Click here to enable desktop notifications for Email Handyman ○ **New mail notifications on** - Notify me when any new mes: ○ **Important mail notifications on** - Notify me only when an ● **Mail notifications off**
Keyboard shortcuts: Learn more	○ **Keyboard shortcuts off** ● **Keyboard shortcuts on**
Button labels: Learn more	● **Icons** ○ **Text**
My picture:	Select a picture that everyone will see when you email them.

Turning on keyboard shortcuts

In Gmail keyboard shortcuts need to be turned on before you can use them. This is done in **Settings** right under the **Desktop Notifications** (see image above).

Archive your old folders

In Gmail folders don't really exist. They are called Labels and do not really bother you anyway. You do want to rename any labels that start with 1, 2, 3 or 4 (perhaps by putting the number at the end of the label name). No further action is required except consciously accepting to stop using the labels.

Add the action folders

1 In Gmail, in the navigation pane on the left click on **More** and then **Create new label**.
2 Type **1 FILED ITEMS** as the label name and hit enter.
3 Repeat this to add the labels **2 DO THIS WEEK**, **3 HOLDING FOR LATER** and **4 WAITING FOR OTHERS**.

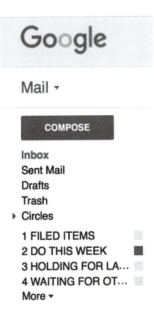

Enter the weekly check into your Calendar

1 Go to Google **Calendar** and select a time slot to do your weekly check (for instance, 9:00 AM to 10:00 AM Friday morning).
2 Enter **Weekly Check** as the subject of the appointment.
3 Click on **Edit** and tick **Repeat** to make it weekly recurring.

4 In the **Description** field type (or copy and paste using Ctrl+C and Ctrl+V) the checklist below, and then save the appointment.

Weekly checklist

- Calendar, past week.
- Calendar, coming week.
- Voicemail.
- Paper notes.
- Do This Week.
- Holding for Later.
- Waiting for Others.

Top 10 keyboard shortcuts for Gmail

- **Enter** => open discussion.
- v => move discussion.
- / => move cursor to 'Search' box.
- c => compose.
- r => reply.
- a => reply to all.
- f => forward.
- **Tab** then **Enter** => send.
- z => undo last action.
- ? => show keyboard shortcuts.

Speedmailing on an iPhone or iPad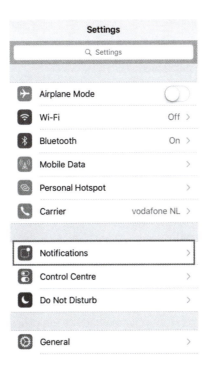

We will assume that cleaning and setting up the folders has already been done as that is easier on a computer and should synchronise to your mobile device.

Turn off new email notifications

To turn off new email notifications on iOS go to **Settings**, **Accounts** and then choose the email account you would like to edit. For each account go to **Account settings**, **Notification settings** and turn off the email notifications.

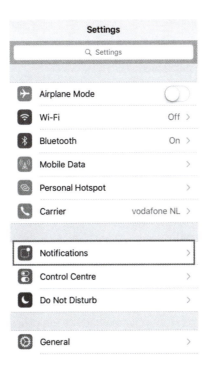

Emptying your inbox

Using your mobile device to empty your inbox can be a great addition to your speedmailing habit. I often crunch my new emails when I have to wait somewhere and don't feel like taking my laptop out.

How do we apply the process on a mobile phone? First of all, we use the same logic, with the exception that a two-minute rule might become a 20-second rule. Anything worth typing out properly can be moved to the 'Do This Week' folder and will be taken care of when back at the office.

So we start at the top, open the email to judge what to do with it and then use one of two buttons. **Delete** or **Move**. As the action folders are on the top of the list it will be quick and easy to process them one by one until your inbox is empty.

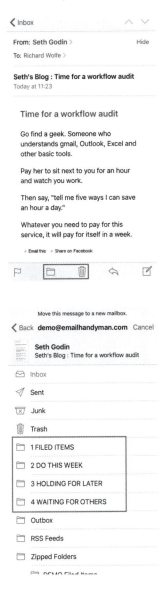

You might find that the list of folders in your iOS device is annoyingly long, which can be caused by deleted folders that are still in your **Deleted Items**. To resolve this, empty your **Deleted Items** in Outlook by right-clicking on the folder and choosing **Empty Folder**.

Keyboard shortcuts

Not the expected list, but a great feature of iOS is the ability to use shortcuts to produce pieces of text. This was known as shortcuts but now carries the name Text Replacements. Some are built in, for instance 'omw' will convert to 'On my way!' You also have the ability to create your own, which is great for frequently used text snippets. For instance, 'kr' can be the shortcut for 'Kind regards, Richard'. An extra bonus if you also use a Mac computer, the Text replacements will sync through iCloud so you can benefit on every keyboard.

To access the shortcuts, go to the **Settings** app, **General**, **Keyboard** and then **Text replacement**.

If you do have an external keyboard please check out our tips on http://shortcuts.emailhandyman.com

iPhone or iPad

Speedmailing on a device for Android

We will assume that cleaning and setting up the folders has already been done as that is easier on a computer and should synchronise to your mobile device.

Turn off new email notifications

To turn off new email notifications on Android, go to the **Email** app, choose **More** and then **Settings**. Scroll down to **Notifications settings** and turn off Email notifications.

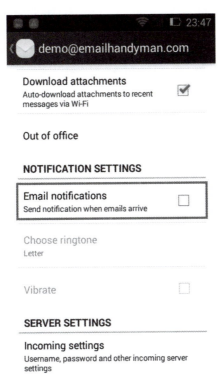

Emptying your inbox

Using your mobile device to empty your inbox can be a great addition to your speedmailing habit. I often crunch my new emails when I have to wait somewhere and don't feel like taking my laptop out.

How do we apply the process on a mobile phone? First of all, we use the same logic, with the exception that a two-minute rule might become a 20-second rule. Anything worth typing out properly can be moved to the 'Do This Week' folder and will be taken care of when back at the office.

So we start at the top, open the email to judge what to do with it and then use the **Delete** or **Move** icon to move the email to the folder of choice.

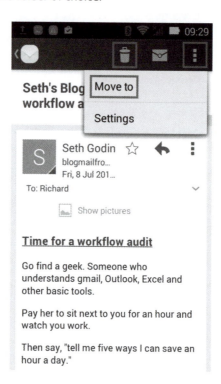

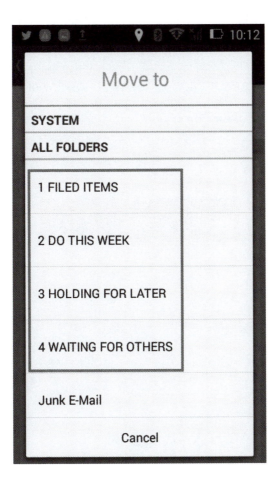

You might find that the list of folders in your Android device is annoyingly long, which can be caused by deleted folders that are still in your **Deleted Items**. To resolve this, empty your **Deleted Items** in Outlook by right-clicking on the folder and choosing **Empty Folder**.

Speedmailing on a Windows phone

We will assume that cleaning and setting up the folders has already been done as that is easier on a computer and should synchronise to your mobile device.

Turn off new email notifications

By default, email notifications are turned off on a Windows phone. If you need to change the setting go to your **Account settings**, click **Manage** and adjust the **Notification settings**.

Emptying your inbox

Using your mobile device to empty your inbox can be a great addition to your speedmailing habit. I often crunch my new emails when I have to wait somewhere and don't feel like taking my laptop out.

How do we apply the process on a mobile phone? First of all, we use the same logic, with the exception that a two-minute rule might become a 20-second rule. Anything worth typing out properly can be moved to the 'Do This Week' folder and will be taken care of when back at the office.

So we start at the top, open the email to judge what to do with it and then use the **Delete** or **Move** icon to move the email to the folder of choice.

SG **Seth Godin**
    08/07/2011 12:27   →

Seth's Blog : Time for a workflow audit
To: Richard Wolfe

Time for a workflow audit

Go find a geek. Someone who
understands gmail, Outlook, Excel and
other basic tools.

Pay her to sit next to you for an hour and
watch you work.

Then say, "tell me five ways I can save an
hour a day."

Whatever you need to pay for this

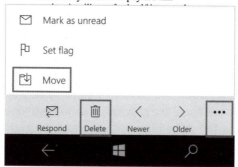

✉ Mark as unread

⚑ Set flag

📤 Move

✉	🗑	‹	›	•••
Respond	Delete	Newer	Older	

←   ⊞   🔍

Windows
phone

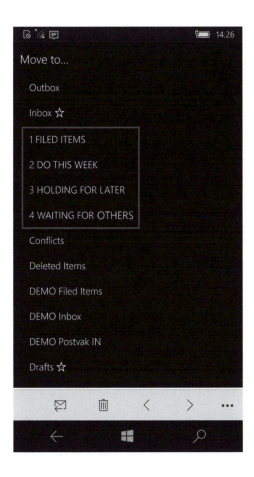

Speedmailing on other platforms

The benefits of speedmailing are not limited to the applications and systems mentioned in this book. We often help people who work with Lotus Notes, GroupWise, BlackBerry devices, etc. Using the Help feature of your client will quickly tell you how to create folders and what keyboard shortcuts are available. In the end it is all about just one trick: how to move an email from one folder to another.

Happy speedmailing!

What did you think of this book?

We're really keen to hear from you about this book, so that we can make our publishing even better.

Please log on to the following website and leave us your feedback.

It will only take a few minutes and your thoughts are invaluable to us.

www.pearsoned.co.uk/bookfeedback

Other platforms

Index